D0527809

Rugby
SPORTS SKILLS

Clive Gifford

W
FRANKLIN WATTS
LONDON•SYDNEY

Franklin Watts
Published in Great Britain in 2017 by
The Watts Publishing Group

Copyright © The Watts Publishing Group
2015

All rights reserved.

Credits
Series Editor: Adrian Cole
Art direction: Peter Scoulding
Series designed and created for
 Franklin Watts by Storeybooks
Designer: Rita Storey
Editor: Nicola Barber
Photography: Tudor Photography,
 Banbury (unless otherwise stated)

Every attempt has been made to clear
copyright. Should there be any inadvertent
omission please apply to the publisher for
rectification.

Dewey number 796.3'33
HB ISBN 978 1 4451 5246 2

Printed in China

MIX
Paper from
responsible sources
FSC® C104740
FSC
www.fsc.org

Franklin Watts
An imprint of Hachette Children's Group
Part of The Watts Publishing Group
Carmelite House
50 Victoria Embankment
London EC4Y 0DZ

An Hachette UK Company
www.hachette.co.uk

www.franklinwatts.co.uk

Note: At the time of going to press, the
statistics and profiles in this book were up to
date. However, due to some cyclists' active
participation in the sport, it is possible that
some of these may now be out of date.

Picture credits
Shutterstock/ Paolo Bona p.6; Sophia Rugby
/Didier Honoré/Wikimedia Commons;
p.7; Martin Hunter/Getty Images p.21;
Shutterstock/ Maxisport p.22; Bradley Kanaris
/Gettyp.25; Shutterstock/ Max Blain p.26;
Shutterstock/ Neil Balderson p. 27.

Cover images: Tudor Photography, Banbury.

All photos posed by models. Thanks to Joel
Avery, Tim Bennett,

Jamie Bache, Carl Daniels, Josh Deegan, Carl
Taylor, Mark Woodward and Jackson Wray.

The Publisher would like to thank The
Publisher would like to thank Banbury RUFC
for the use of the club's ground.

Previously published by Franklin Watts as
Know Your Sport Rugby.

Taking part in sport is a fun
way to get fit, but like any
form of physical exercise it has
an element of risk, particularly
if you are unfit, overweight
or suffer from any medical
conditions. It is advisable
to consult a healthcare
professional before beginning
any programme of exercise.

Contents

Introduction

Rugby is a tough, all-action game played between two teams. It is great to watch and even more fun to play.

It comes in many versions but all of them feature an oval ball that players carry in their hands, pass or kick. The two teams try to score points while preventing their opponents from scoring points against them.

Aim of the Game

The two teams try to gain points by scoring 'tries'. A try is scored when a player grounds the ball in the in-goal area (see page 8) of the opposing team. When a team scores a try it has the chance to add extra points with a 'conversion'. This is scored by one player kicking the ball between the goalposts. Teams can also score points through penalty kicks and drop goals.

Fourie du Preez of South Africa passes the ball during the 2007 World Cup final against England. South Africa went on to win the championship.

● It's a Fact

Teams in the men's World Cup compete for the William Webb Ellis Trophy. It is named after a pupil at Rugby School, in England, who was playing a game of football in 1823 when he picked up the ball and ran with it in his hands. Many believe this was how rugby began.

Rugby for All

Rugby union is open to players of all shapes and sizes. It is also played at all age and ability levels. Many rugby clubs run teams ranging from under-10s to over-40s. Women's and girls' rugby is also booming in popularity. For the world's best players, the most important competition is the World Cup, which is held separately for men and women. It is played every four years.

Junior Games

Rugby union is a 15-a-side game played over two halves of 40 minutes each. Smaller-scale versions of the game, played for shorter times and featuring fewer players, exist for younger players. These include tag rugby, which is a non-contact version of the sport, and mini rugby. In some countries, girls and boys play mini and tag rugby together until the age of 11.

The History of Rugby

In the 19th century, different versions of football and rugby football emerged.

In 1871, clubs met to draw up an agreed way of playing and formed the Rugby Football Union. Arguments about professionalism (being paid to play) raged within the Union and in 1895, 22 rugby clubs in the north of England formed the Northern Rugby Football Union, which was later renamed the Rugby Football League. Both Union and League have developed different rules and ways of playing (see pages 24–27). This book concentrates on rugby union.

In tag rugby, a player is 'tackled' when an opponent manages to pull away a ribbon from the player's belt. The tackler then steps back and the tackled player must pass the ball.

World Cup Victory

In 2014, England ended a run of three successive final defeats to win the Women's Rugby World Cup in Paris.

Players, Pitch and Positions

A full-sized rugby pitch is up to 69 metres wide and 100 metres long, with two in-goal areas of a maximum depth of 22 metres. The 15 players on each side are divided into eight forwards (the players who form scrums – see page 26) and seven backs.

Forwards (1–8)
1 Loose-head prop
2 Hooker
3 Tight-head prop
4 and 5 Lock forwards
6 and 7 Flankers
8 No. 8

Backs (9–15)
9 Scrum-half
10 Fly-half (also known as stand-off)
11 Winger
12 Inside centre
13 Outside centre
14 Winger
15 Full-back

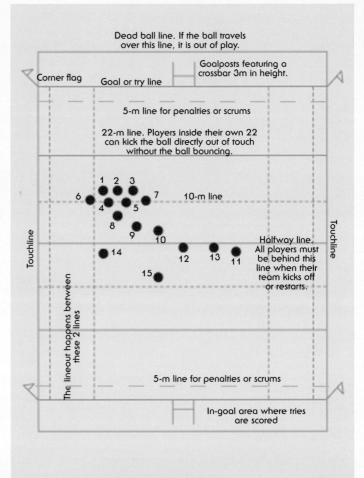

Dead ball line. If the ball travels over this line, it is out of play.

Corner flag

Goalposts featuring a crossbar 3m in height.

Goal or try line

5-m line for penalties or scrums

22-m line. Players inside their own 22 can kick the ball directly out of touch without the ball bouncing.

10-m line

Touchline

Touchline

Halfway line. All players must be behind this line when their team kicks off or restarts.

The lineout happens between these 2 lines

5-m line for penalties or scrums

In-goal area where tries are scored

Forwards and Backs

Forwards are involved in scrums and lineouts (see pages 26–27) and generally in winning the ball for their side. They feed the ball to the scrum-half and fly-half who have the choice of kicking the ball, running with it or passing it out to the backs.

Forwards tend to be larger, heavier and slower than backs, though the difference between them is becoming less and less In modern rugby forwards need to be able to move around the pitch quickly, while backs need to be strong enough to surge through tackles and defend well.

Referees and Rules

The referee is in charge of the rugby match and makes decisions that have to be followed by all the players. The referee is assisted by two touch judges. They run up and down the touchline during the game, and also stand beneath the goalposts when a penalty kick or conversion is taken. In some top-flight rugby league and union games, there is an additional official, known as the video referee. If a try is in dispute, for example, the match referee can signal to the video referee to give a ruling.

Rugby is a technical game with many complicated rules. Players need to learn all the laws of rugby. You should discuss any you are unsure about with your coach.

The Referee's Signals

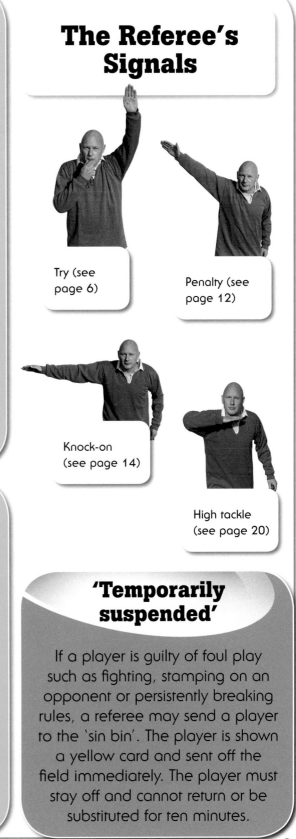

Try (see page 6)

Penalty (see page 12)

Knock-on (see page 14)

High tackle (see page 20)

Restarts

Each half of a match is started with a kick-off taken from, or behind, the centre of the halfway line. Kick-offs are also used to restart the game after a try is scored. The ball must travel over the opponents' 10-m line and stay in play. If not, the opposing team can order the kick to be re-taken or can choose to have a scrum (see page 26) at the centre of the halfway line. Another type of restart, the 22-m drop out, is a drop kick (see page 22) taken from behind the 22-m line.

'Temporarily suspended'

If a player is guilty of foul play such as fighting, stamping on an opponent or persistently breaking rules, a referee may send a player to the 'sin bin'. The player is shown a yellow card and sent off the field immediately. The player must stay off and cannot return or be substituted for ten minutes.

Training and Kit

Rugby is a fast and physical game. Players need to be very fit to perform at their best. Rugby can also be a dangerous game. To avoid injury, players need to prepare for matches thoroughly and always obey the referee's instructions.

A Player's Kit

Players in the same team wear identical strips. New developments in fabric technology have meant that rugby kit has changed a great deal in the past few years. Lightwight warm fabrics that 'wick' moisture away from the body means that shirts can be closer fitting but still comfortable to wear. This new kit also gives an opponent less fabric to grab hold of! Boots (ideally with adjustable screw-in studs) should fit comfortably and laces should be securely tied. A tracksuit to keep warm before and after a game is also important.

Stretching

Rugby players perform a series of stretches to the key muscles in their legs, arms and back before starting a game. These stretches help them perform at their best and prevent injuries.

Protection

Players can also choose to wear:

- lightweight shinpads to protect the front of their legs
- a padded headguard, called a scrum cap, for head and ear protection
- a correctly fitted gumshield.

Fitness

Adult players do strength and conditioning exercises in a gym. Being physically fit when you play rugby helps to avoid injury. The exercises are designed for the position they play.

Junior players need to concentrate on developing their overall fitness. They can do this by:

- playing other physical sports, such as football
- attending training sessions
- eating healthily.

Skills

Adult players practise the core skills of passing, catching, running and tackling over and over again throughout their playing career.

As well as attending regular training sessions junior players can practice passing and catching, swerves and sidesteps (see pages 12–15 and 18–19) with a couple of friends in a park.

Many injuries occur during tackles, especially if a player tackles with poor technique. This young player is practising safely by using a tackle bag under the watchful eye of his coach.

Passing

Passing links a team's play together. The ball must be thrown backwards or sideways but never forwards, which is against the rules. If a player deliberately passes the ball forwards, the referee may award a penalty. If it is thrown forwards accidentally, the referee orders a scrum (see page 26) at the place where the pass was made.

The Lateral Pass

The Lateral Pass

This is the most basic and the most common pass in rugby and is an essential part of every rugby player's skills. Top players continue to practise their passing throughout their careers. Accuracy is very important. When you and the person receiving the pass are moving forwards, you have to judge where the receiver will be by the time the pass arrives. You should make that your target, aiming the ball so that the receiver catches the ball at chest height.

The ball needs to be thrown with the right amount of force and the timing of the pass is crucial.

1 The player looks for the person to whom he is passing. He holds the ball at chest height in both hands. Only his fingers are in contact with the surface of the ball.

2 The passer swings his arms across his body towards the receiver. His rear hand pushes the ball while the other hand guides it in the right direction.

3 As the ball leaves his hands, the passer flicks his wrists and fingers. This puts some spin on the ball, which helps it to fly directly towards the target. The player follows through with his arms and fingers pointing towards the target.

• An Olympic Sport

In 2009 the Olympic committee voted to include Rugby Sevens, a style of rugby with seven players on each team, as an Olympic sport from 2016.

The passer (left) watches both the receiver (far right) and the opponent closing in. He must time his pass well.

Short pass

To throw a short lateral pass:

- hold the ball at about chest height
- flick your fingers and wrists to 'pop' the ball up and towards the receiver.

Long pass

A good, long pass can open up a game and release players in plenty of space to run forward. There is a risk that the ball might be intercepted by an opponent, so throw a long pass only if there is space and you are confident of your accuracy.

To send a long lateral pass:

- swing your shoulders and twist at the waist to add power.

Passing Drill

Passing and catching should be practised at every opportunity. Many beginners find it far easier to pass in one direction than the other. Players should work hard on their weaker side so that they can pass from either hand.

- In this drill three players stand in a row a few metres apart and run and pass the ball between them.
- The middle player passes and receives the ball in both directions.
- Switch over the player in the middle as you repeat the drill.

Corridor Drill

Walk through this drill a few times before gradually building up speed.

- In an area, or 'corridor', 10m to 12m wide, two players repeatedly pass the ball to each other, making sure not to pass the ball forwards.
- The defender cannot tackle the players, but can try to intercept the ball.
- If the ball is intercepted, dropped or goes outside the corridor, the defender changes places with one of the passers.

Catching

Catching the ball is just as important as passing it. If you fail to catch the ball, your opponents may gain possession, putting your team in danger of conceding a try.

Knock-on

A fumbled catch may result in the referee signalling a 'knock-on'. This is when a player fails to catch the ball, fumbles it forwards and it touches the ground. When this happens, a referee awards a scrum (see page 26) to the opposing team. It is not a knock-on if a player fumbles the ball but catches it at the second attempt before it touches the ground.

Safe Hands

Always stay alert so that ready to receive a pass If possible, try to take the two hands and then pull into your body to protect

Always be prepared for a ba that does not arrive at the ideal height. You may have to bend and stretch to catch a low ball, or reach up high.

Catching

1 The receiver (right) is in a position to receive a pass, his eyes are focused on the passer. When the ball is released, the receiver's hands are at chest height, with his thumbs up and fingers spread. This helps create a target for the pass.

2 The receiver keeps hi the ball. As the pass arriv player extends his hands the ball without over-stre gets a good grip on the brings his hands in and cushion its landing.

Taking a High Ball on the Ground

1 The player calls to his team-mates that he is going to take the catch. Keeping his eyes on the ball, he gets into position to catch it. He spreads his feet apart to help his balance and raises his arms, fingers spread and pointing upwards.

2 As the player catches the ball, he cushions it by bringing his arms down towards his chest. The player crouches and turns his body to protect the ball from approaching opponents.

In the Air

Sometimes you may need to jump to catch a high ball. You cannot be tackled while you are in the air. If an opponent tries to tackle you when your feet are off the ground, the referee should award your team a penalty. If you catch the ball in your own 22-m area, you can call a 'mark' – literally by shouting "Mark!" as you catch it. When you do this, the players in the other team have to retreat 10m, your team-mates fall in behind you, and you are awarded a free-kick.

Ball-handling

As part of their preparations before a game, players practise passing and catching to get a feel for the ball. This is especially important if the conditions are wet or windy, or if it is very cold. You can practise some elements of ball-handling by yourself. Throw the ball up and over to one side of your shoulders and then twist at the waist to collect it securely at chest height. Throw the ball higher and straight up and get underneath it to practise your high catching.

Timing Runs

Instead of kicking or passing the ball, players may see some space ahead and decide to run with the ball themselves. Players need to know when and how to make attacking runs with the ball and, importantly, how to support their team's attack by making runs without the ball.

Running with the Ball

Every running situation in a rugby match is different, but there are key things you should do every time you run with the ball.

- Protect the ball by keeping it close to your chest.
- Keep your head up and be aware of how play is developing around you. Has a gap appeared? Are opponents closing in? Is there a team-mate in a better position to whom you can pass? Should you kick ahead or into touch?

Supporting Runs

The player with the ball is called the ball-carrier. Good teams try to not let their ball-carrier become isolated on the pitch.

If the ball-carrier is about to be tackled, team-mates give the player options for a pass. If tackled, they will also offer support to try to keep possession of the ball.

In attack, team-mates try to make runs at different angles to split and disrupt the other team's defence.

Overlap Play

Through passing and running with the ball, teams seek to create an attacking situation where they have more players ready to receive the ball than there are defenders to guard or tackle them. One example of this is the overlap.

This player has his head up and his eyes focused on a gap into which he wants to sprint. He holds the ball securely in both hands.

The Overlap

1 The ball-carrier runs hard but is aware of a defender closing in on him. Meanwhile, his team-mate is starting a fast run down the touchline to create an overlap.

2 The defender is caught in two minds over whether to tackle the ball-carrier or to follow the wide runner. The ball-carrier waits for the right moment to pass. If it is too late, the receiver may be ahead of him. If it is too early, the defender may anticipate the pass and intercept the ball.

3 The defender has been drawn towards the ball-carrier, who releases the pass at the right moment. The receiver collects the pass and is free to run down the touchline.

Beating an Opponent

The easiest way to beat an opponent is to pass the ball to a team-mate, but there are also some situations where you need to keep hold of the ball and go past an opponent. When it is done well, beating an opponent using speed and surprise is one of the most exhilarating moments in rugby.

Change of Pace and Direction

Changes of pace and direction are simple but effective ways of getting past an opponent. A decrease in your running speed, together with a slight change of direction in your running line, may cause a defender to hesitate and give you the chance to sprint away.

The Dummy Move

A dummy is when you pretend to pass to a team-mate to fool one or more defenders but you actually keep hold of the ball. For it to work well your movements have to be convincing and there has to be a team-mate in close support.

The Dummy

1 If the defender does not commit to tackling the ball-carrier, the ball-carrier turns his head to his team-mate and goes through all the movements of making a pass but keeps a firm grip on the ball.

2 The defender is deceived into believing that the ball-carrier is about to pass and makes a move to tackle his team-mate. The ball-carrier quickly changes his running angle away from the defender and increases his pace to sprint away.

The Sidestep

A sidestep is useful to get past an opponent. To perform a sidestep, this player puts all his weight on his right foot and then drives off that foot to change direction towards his left. Performed well, a sidestep can fool a defender into moving in the wrong direction.

The Swerve

Harder to learn, the swerve is a more dramatic change of direction.

- Approach the defender straight on with the ball in both hands.
- Three or four paces before you reach the defender, lean sharply to one side and make your next stride across your body.
- Use the edges of your boots to lean away and swerve around the player.

- Sprint away as straight and as fast as you can once past the defender

The Scissors or Switch Pass

Another way that two team-mates can beat a defender is the scissors pass or switch pass. The player with the ball runs towards the defender, but just before the tackle, the ball-carrier twists the upper body and passes to a team-mate.

The Scissors or Switch Pass

1 The ball-carrier (right) needs support from a team-mate running in the opposite diagonal direction behind him.

2 Just before the two cross, the ball-carrier twists at the waist and releases a short, gentle pass. The receiver (left) collects the ball and sprints away.

Tackling

Tackling is a key part of defence. It should be practised often, under the supervision of your coach. Tackling with the correct technique will result in fewer injuries.

Tackle Talk

Tackling is more about skill and technique than brute strength. Good technique will allow smaller players to tackle bigger and heavier players. Apart from learning tackling techniques, players must know the rules about tackling. For example, you should never stick out a foot to trip an opponent or make a high tackle around the neck or head. Both are against the rules of rugby and could be very dangerous. Nor should you make a late or early tackle, where you tackle a player who does not have the ball.

Side-on Tackle

The side-on tackle is one of the most common tackles in a game. Many coaches of junior players believe that it is also the best tackle to learn first.

1 The tackler (in blue) focuses on the opponent with the ball, aiming to make contact just above waist height. This is where his shoulder will impact with the player.

2 The tackler drives off on the leg on the same side of the body as the shoulder making the impact. He uses his full body weight to hit his opponent. He must make sure that his head slips behind the player being tackled and not in front. This helps avoid injuries.

Tap Tackle

A tap tackle can be used when an opponent is out of reach of a full tackle. Use an outstretched arm to give one of your opponent's ankles a firm tap. This can knock a player off balance or cause them to stumble and fall.

Defending

There is more to defending than just tackling. All the players in a team should defend as a single unit. If your opponent gets past you, do not give up but sprint back hard. A team-mate may have slowed down his attack and you could be needed to help out or make another tackle. Spread out across the pitch to protect your territory and try line. Defenders look to cut down the space the ball-carrier and his supporting team-mates have. Defenders must also stay alert to opponents running into danger areas, or an unexpected kick above or behind them.

Richie McCaw

New Zealand
Date of birth: 31 December, 1980
Position: Flanker
Height: 1.88m
Weight: 106kg
International caps: 148
International points: 135

Richie Hugh McCaw has been captain of the New Zealand All Blacks team over 100 times. Under his captaincy the team have been one of the most dominant sports teams in history, winning 97 of their 110 games. The South African rugby coach, Heyneke Meyer, said of McCaw 'He is probably the best player who has ever played rugby.'

3 As he makes impact, the tackler wraps his arms around his opponent's legs and holds firmly. He and his opponent fall to the ground.

Kicking

There are many types of kick in rugby union. Some are to score points, such as the penalty kick or the drop kick aimed between the posts. Other kicks are used to improve a team's position, to set up an attack or to clear the ball into touch.

Drop Kicks

Drop kicks are used for some restarts and when trying to score a drop goal. To perform a drop kick, begin with the ball in your hands. Then release the ball and as it touches the ground, swing your foot through the ball, finishing with a high follow-through. It is important to keep your head down, your eyes on the ball and your weight on your non-kicking foot.

Jonny Wilkinson

England
Date of birth: 25 May, 1979
Position: Fly-half
Height: 1.78m
Weight: 89kg
International caps: 97
International points: 1246

Wilkinson will always be remembered for his drop kick against Australia in the last minute of extra time that won England the 2003 World Cup. He is England's leading all-time points-scorer but is more than just a phenomenally accurate goalkicker. He is deceptively quick, an astute passer and a ferocious tackler. A long-serving member of the Newcastle Falcons club, he suffered from numerous injury problems after the 2003 World Cup. He recovered to be selected for the 2005 British and Irish Lions tour of New Zealand but struggled to rediscover his old form. He retired from rugby in 2014.

The Drop Kick

In a drop kick, the kicker aims to make contact a third of the way from the bottom of the ball just as it reaches the ground. This should lift the ball high into the air. You can take turns to practise drop kicks with a friend on the other side the posts.

Goal Kick

1 With the ball pointing upwards or lined up towards the target on a mound of dirt, or a plastic kicking tee, the kicker starts his approach. His head is down and his eyes are focused on the ball.

2 The kicker places his non-kicking foot 10–20cm to the side of the ball and slightly behind it. He supports his bodyweight on this leg and keeps his head over the ball as his kicking leg swings through the ball.

3 The instep (where the boot laces are) makes contact about a third of the way up the ball. The kicker's leg follows through in front and slightly across his body.

Goalkicking

Goalkicking is used for conversions and for penalty kicks. All goalkickers have their own way of lining up a kick and how many paces they take to the ball. Work with your coach to find out what suits you best.

Grubber Kicks

The grubber kick is a low, stabbed or punched kick that causes the ball to roll end-over-end along the ground. It can be used to put the ball into touch when outside of the 22-m area, and to nudge the ball forwards and past the opposition defence for a team-mate to sprint on to and collect. Make sure your body is over the ball and aim for your laces to hit the upper half of the ball, keeping your leg low and straight in the follow-through.

Punts and Other Kicks

Other kicks used in rugby union include the long punt, which is often used by a fly-half or full-back to kick the ball into touch. It is similar to a drop kick, but the player's boot makes contact with the ball before the ball touches the ground. There is also the high kick, known as a 'Garryowen' or an 'up-and-under'. This is kicked in a similar way to the punt but hoisted high into the air. The aim is to put the opposition team under pressure as you and your team-mates chase the kick.

Union and League Differences 1

Rugby union and rugby league differ in a number of ways, such as the number of players in each team and the rules about tackling.

After the Tackle: Rugby Union

When a player is tackled in rugby union, a complicated set of rules apply. The tackled player must let go of the ball or risk giving away a penalty. A ruck occurs when the ball is on the ground and competing players from both teams are in physical contact. In a ruck, only players on their feet can handle the ball.

Key Rule Differences

	Rugby Union	Rugby League
Number of players	15	13
Points for a try	5	4
Points for a drop goal	3	1
Points for a penalty kick	3	2
Numbers of players in scrum	8	6

Collecting the Ball: Rugby Union

The tackled player has managed to turn back facing his try line and places the ball at arm's length. His supporting team-mate is the first to arrive. He steps over the ball and bends his knees to get low as he collects the ball.

Mauls: Rugby Union

A maul is another move that can occur after a tackle. A maul can form when:

- a player has been tackled but keeps hold of the ball;
- is in physical contact with an opponent, but stays on his feet;
- is supported by team-mates who must join from behind.

These players maintain contact driving forward on their feet until either a player breaks away with the ball or a pass is made.

After the Tackle: Rugby League

In rugby league, a tackler must get off the player they have tackled quickly or risk giving away a penalty. The tackled player then plays the ball. This is done by placing the ball on the ground and rolling it backwards with a foot. A team-mate can then pick up the ball and play it.

Six Tackles: Rugby League

When players from the same team are tackled six times in a row, possession of the ball passes to the opposing team. Teams drive up the pitch in the first few tackles. As the sixth tackle approaches, a team can kick the ball deep into the other team's half to gain territorial advantage. If the players are near their opponents' try line when the sixth tackle approaches, they

may continue running and passing or place a short kick into their opponents' in-goal area in the hope of scoring a try.

Johnathan Thurston

Australia
Date of Birth: 25 April, 1983
Position: Halfback, Five-eighth
Height 1.79m
Weight: 86kg

Johnathan Dean Thurston is an indigenous Australian professional rugby league player. Despite being an outstanding school and club player he struggled to find a national rugby league club willing to sign him because of his small size. Eventually he was signed by Canterbury-Bankstown Bulldogs. He has achieved the highest individual honour in rugby league by being awarded the Golden Boot World Player of the Year title in 2011. He is also top point-scorer with 372 points scored while representing Australia (The Kangaroos).

Union and League Differences 2

The different codes of rugby have different ways of restarting the game after it has been stopped. In rugby union, two of these restarts – the scrum and the lineout – form important parts of the game.

Scrums: Rugby League

In rugby league, when the ball goes over the touchline, a scrum is taken level with where it went out. A scrum may also be awarded when a team knocks on or throws a forward pass. The rugby league scrum lines up with three in the front row, two in the second and one in the third. The ball is fed in by the scrum-half and the middle player in the front row tries to hook (strike) the ball backwards.

A rugby league scrum during a match between the Sydney Roosters and the New Zealand Warriors in the NRL. A Rooster player (in white) has just received the ball from the scrum and gets ready to pass it.

Warning: Scrums

Scrums can be dangerous because of the enormous weight and power involved. Never practise scrums without an experienced coach on hand.

Scrums: Rugby Union

In a rugby union scrum, eight forwards line up in a 3-2-3 formation, binding together in set ways. Following the referee's commands, the two sets of forwards lock together, or 'engage'.

The scrum-half from the team in possession feeds the ball down the tunnel between the two front rows. His hooker aims to strike the ball, rolling it back to the feet of the No. 8, the player at the back of the scrum. This player controls the ball with his feet. He can keep it under control as the scrum moves forwards, pick it up and run with it, or let it out of the scrum for his scrum-half to pick up and pass.

Lineouts: Rugby Union

Lineouts occur only in rugby union. They take place when the ball crosses the touchline and goes out of play. The team that did not touch the ball last throws the ball in at the lineout. An exception is when a team is awarded a penalty and kicks the ball into touch. In this case, the kicking team gets the throw-in. Up to seven forwards from each team line up between 5m and 15m from the touchline. The throw-in is taken by the hooker, who judges the length, height and timing of his throw so that his team's 'jumpers' have the best chance of reaching the ball before their opponents. The throw must be straight, or the referee will halt play. The jumpers may catch the ball or knock it back to their scrum-half.

England player (in white) Geoff Parling jumps for the ball in a lineout during a 2012 match between England and South Africa at Twickenham, London.

27

Statistics and Records

Rugby Union

Rugby World Cup Results
1991 Australia 12 England 6
1995 South Africa 15 New Zealand 12
1999 Australia 35 France 12
2003 England 20 Australia 17
2007 South Africa 15 Engand 6
2011 New Zealand 8 France 7
2015 New Zealand 34 Australia 17

Women's World Cup Results
1991 USA 19 England 6
1994 England 38 USA 23
1998 New Zealand 44 USA 12
2002 New Zealand 19 England 9
2006 New Zealand 25 England 17
2010 New Zealand 13 England 10
2014 England 21 Canada 9

Most International Appearances
Richie McCaw (New Zealand) 148
Brian O'Driscoll (Ireland/Lions) 141
George Gregan (Australia) 139
Ronan O'Gara (Ireland/Lions) 130

Most International Drop Goals
Jonny Wilkinson (England/Lions) 36
Hugo Porta (Argentina) 28
Rob Andrew (England) 23
Diego Dominguez (Argentina/Italy) 20

All Time International Points Scorer
Dan Carter (New Zeland) 1598
Jonny Wilkinson (England/Lions) 1246
Neil Jenkins (Wales/Lions) 1090
Ronan O'Gara (Ireland/Lions) 1083
Diego Dominguez (Argentina/Italy) 1010
Andrew Mehrtens (New Zealand) 994
Michael Lynagh (Australia) 911

Top International Try Scorers
Daisuke Ohata (Japan) 69
Bryan Habana (South Africa) 67
David Campese (Australia) 64

Highest Attendance at a Match
109,874 at Stadium Australia, Sydney
(July 2000)
for Australia v New Zealand

Rugby League

World Cup Results
1977 Australia 13 Great Britain 12
1988 Australia 25 New Zealand 12
1992 Australia 10 Great Britain 6
1995 Australia 16 England 8
2000 Australia 40 New Zealand 12
2008 New Zealand 34 Australia 20
2013 Australia 34 New Zealand 2

Australian National Rugby League Record
Most grand final wins (club) 21 – Souths
Most tries in a career 212 – Ken Irvine
Most points in a career 2418 – Hazem
El Masri
Leading points-scorer in a season: 342
– Hazem El Masri (2004)

Glossary

Backs The seven players who line up behind the scrum.

Ball-carrier The player holding the ball.

Conversion A kick awarded after a try. The ball must travel between the posts and over the crossbar. A successful conversion is worth two points in rugby union and in rugby league.

Drop goal A kick from the hand betwen the goal posts to score three points.

Drop kick A kick where the ball is dropped and kicked as it lands on the ground.

Dummy pass Pretending to make a pass by going right through the passing movement but retaining the ball and aiming to send the defender the wrong way.

Forward pass A pass that is thrown forward to another player.

Forwards The eight players who form scrums and contest lineouts.

Knock-on When the ball touches the hand or arm of a player and is knocked forward and touches the ground.

Lineout A set piece where forwards line up in parallel lines and the ball is thrown in from the touchline for players to catch or knock back to their scrum-half.

Overlap An attacking situation where attackers outnumber defenders.

Penalty A way of punishing deliberate misconduct by giving the advantage to the opposing team.

Possession Having the ball under control.

Scrum A set piece where usually eight players a side (six in rugby league) link together.

Sidestep A sudden change of forward direction used by the ball-carrier to get past a defender.

Tackle Grabbing hold of the player with the ball so that they are brought to the ground.

Tap tackle A firm tap of the opponent's ankles by a defender's hand.

Touchline The lines marking the side edges of the pitch.

Try A scoring move worth five points in rugby union and four in rugby league.

Websites

www.worldrugby.org
The official website of World Rugby, the organisation that runs international rugby, including the World Cup. You can download a copy of the laws of the game from this website.

www.rbs6nations.com
The official website of the Six Nations Championship.

www.englandrugby.com
The official website of England Rugby.

www.rugby.com.au
A news and information-packed Australian website. Its community section contains short guides for younger players on, for example, techniques, history and mini rugby and other versions of the game.

www.planetrugby.co.uk
A website with coverage of leagues, cups and national teams from all over the world.

www.therfl.co.uk
The website of the Governing Body of Rugby League in England.

www.nrl.com
The website of the Australian National Rugby League.

Note to parents and teachers: every effort has been made by the Publishers to ensure that these websites are suitable for children, that they are of the highest educational value, and that they contain no inappropriate or offensive material. However, because of the nature of the Internet, it is impossible to guarantee that the contents of these sites will not be altered. We strongly advise that Internet access is supervised by a responsible adult.

Index